Sock Odyssey

Kay Gardiner and Ann Shayne

INTRODUCTION

KNITTING A SOCK is one of the most satisfying adventures in all of knitting. It's a quick trip to an amazing three-dimensional reward, and it never gets old. Socks are such a great way to try out a new technique, a new construction, a new weight of yarn.

Who's got socks dancing in her head? Say hello to the extremely clever Fatimah Hinds, a designer who is all about the puzzle of knitting. With a background in earth and atmospheric science, along with a master's degree in middle childhood math and science education, she has an analytical mind—she's an endless experimenter. This Field Guide is a window into Fatimah's imagination.

For the designs here, Fatimah turns to DK-weight yarn to create socks that are cushy, snuggly, and—no small thing—faster to make than the more typical fingering-weight socks.

These are the socks that can stay home and never leave the comfort of your own bed. Or they can be a beautiful extra to wear when you head out.

In this Field Guide, you'll find four patterns with cool techniques to explore.

Toe-Up or Cuff-Down. Fatimah shows us how to work in either direction.

An innovative patch method for beginning a toe-up sock, one that makes for a simple start. In both stockinette and reverse stockinette, it's a magic trick.

Cables. Fatimah gives us six simple cable stitches that can be used in multitudinous combinations.

Lace. Fatimah focuses on simple openwork stitches to yield modern, graphic effects.

A smooth sole. Fatimah has us knit the sole of the sock in reverse stockinette so the smooth side ends up on the inside— so comfy on the foot.

A clever heel. Fatimah sets us up with a tidy heel construction that happens after the leg and foot are complete.

Shaping. Fatimah's Toe-Up Knee Socks are a show-stopping design that allows for a careful fit all the way to the knee.

Let the adventure begin.

Love,

Kay   Ann

Cuff

Leg

Heel

Instep

Sole

Toe

GETTING READY

BEFORE WE START our journey into the land of socks, let's orient ourselves. In the photo at left, we have labeled the key sock regions. And below are pointers to help you plan the adventure.

—Size: To feel good on your foot, your sock needs to fit snugly, so it is important to make it smaller than your foot and leg. (A sock that is too loose will bunch up and sag.) To choose the right size, measure your foot length and your foot circumference (at the ball of the foot). Subtract 10% from each measurement (this is called negative ease), then use the resulting measurements to choose the correct size in the pattern.

—Cuff-down or toe-up: Either you cast on a cuff's worth of stitches (cuff-down) or a few stitches (toe-up). If you are worried you might run short of yarn, it is safer to start at the toe and knit the foot first. The leg of a sock can be long or short, but there is no scrimping on the foot.

— Cable stitch pattern: You'll find instructions for six cable patterns on pages 38–40. These can be used with any of the four patterns in this Field Guide; they're interchangeable. When the pattern indicates it's time to work a cable, pick one and go.

—Cable needles: Fatimah rarely uses them and encourages us to try making cables without a cable needle. It's faster, easy to do, and means you'll never lose a cable needle in the sofa cushions.

—Needle choice: The four patterns in this Field Guide call for double-pointed needles, but feel free to try other types. Options include two circulars; Magic Loop, using one long circular needle; Addi FlexiFlips, which are a set of short, flexible needles; and tiny-circumference circular needles. Ann learned to knit socks on two circular needles with the help of Cat Bordhi's classic book *Socks Soar on Two Circular Needles*.

A note on heels: The method of heel shaping used here results in a longer heel than for most other methods, so if you've made socks before, it may look different to you at first. The longer heel makes for a more comfortable fit where the front of the ankle meets the top of the foot.

Finally, we offer some words of wisdom. As with GPS directions, take your sock instructions as they come, not all at once. Trust the pattern!

CUFF-DOWN YAK-SILK SOCKS

Design by
Fatimah Hinds

C UFF-DOWN SOCKS are great when we want to try out a cable pattern right at the beginning. It's nice to get a good rhythm going.

As elegant a design as you could imagine. Fatimah begins the cables right at the top of the cuff—a sweet design element and a departure from the familiar ribbed cuff. Cable A is the star in the photo at left, and Cables D and E take center stage on page 13.

Why do these socks feel incredible? The yarn. This is Serendipitous Wool's exquisite blend of superwash merino, yak, and silk—all natural fibers, soft as well as sturdy. The colors are especially rich thanks to the natural beige yak base.

KNITTED MEASUREMENTS

Foot Circumference (measured at ball of foot): 7 (8, 9, 10.25)" [18 (20.5, 23, 26) cm]
Foot Length: 9 (10, 11, 11.5)" [23 (25.5, 28, 29) cm]
Leg Length: 6" (10 cm)

SIZES

1 (2, 3, 4)

MATERIALS

— Agni Y by Serendipitous Wool [100 g skeins, each approx. 231 yds (211 m), 60% superwash merino / 20% yak / 20% silk]: 2 skeins Red Earth or Beautyberry
— Size US 4 (3.5 mm) double-point needles (set of 4 or 5), or size needed to achieve gauge
— Stitch markers
— Cable needle
— Waste yarn

GAUGE

23 sts and 32 rnds = 4" (10 cm) over rev st st
Note: Rev st st is not used for the entire sock. The cable pattern will draw the fabric in to the finished measurements.

NOTES

You may choose your cable pattern from among the six given on pages 38–40; they all have the same stitch multiple. The cable patterns may be worked from charts or written text.

The socks are worked from the cuff down. The sole and heel are worked in reverse stockinette so that the smooth side of the knitting is against the foot. The heel is worked inside out.

Traditional cable knitting calls for the use of a third needle, a short little cable needle. If you'd like to learn how to knit cables without a cable needle, which is faster and less fiddly, check out the videos from Emily and Alexa of Tin Can Knits.

LEG

Cast on 52 (60, 68, 76) sts. Distribute sts among 3 or 4 dpns with half of the sts on the first 1 or 2 needles (these will become the instep) and the other half on 2 needles (these will become the heel). Join, being careful not to twist sts; pm for beg of rnd and work in the rnd as follows:

— *Set-Up Rnd 1:* P2 (4, 2, 4), [pm, k6, pm, p2] 2 (2, 3, 3) times, pm, k6, pm, p2 (4, 2, 4), pm for side, p2 (4, 2, 4), [pm, k6, pm, p2] 2 (2, 3, 3) times, pm, k6, pm, p2 (4, 2, 4).

— *Set-Up Rnd 2:* *Purl to marker, [sm, work Cable Chart over 6 sts, sm, p2] 2 (2, 3, 3) times, sm, work Cable Chart over 6 sts, sm, purl to next marker, sm; rep from * to end.

— Work even until piece measures 6" [15 cm] or to desired leg length to top of heel.

HEEL OPENING

— *Next Rnd:* Work in established pattern to side marker, sm, purl to end.

— *Next Rnd:* Work in established pattern to side marker, sm, drop working yarn and purl across sole sts with waste yarn, cut waste yarn; slide sole sts back to left needle and purl across sole sts with working yarn.

FOOT

— *Next Rnd:* Work in established pattern to side marker, sm, purl to end.

— Work even until foot measures 5 (6, 7, 7.5)" [12.5 (15, 18, 19) cm], or to approx 4" (10 cm) less than desired length from waste yarn. This allows for 2" (5 cm) each for toe and heel shaping.

TOE

— Work in pattern to side marker, sm, knit to end.

— *Dec Rnd:* K1, ssk, work in pattern to 3 sts before side marker, k2tog, k1, sm, k1, ssk, knit to last 3 sts, k2tog, k1—4 sts dec.

— Continuing to work in pattern as established on instep sts and in st st on sole sts, rep Dec Rnd every 3 rnds 4 more times—32 (40, 48, 56) sts.

— Knit 2 rnds.

— Graft toe sts (see page 41).

HEEL

Turn the sock inside out. Carefully remove waste yarn and place 26 (30, 34, 38) top and bottom sts each onto 3 or 4 dpns. Rejoin yarn to top sts; pm for beg of rnd and work in the rnd as follows:

— *Set-Up Rnd:* Knit to end of top sts, pick up and knit 1 st tbl from corner, pm, knit across bottom sts, pick up and knit 1 st tbl from corner—54 (62, 70, 78) sts.

— *Dec Rnd:* K1, ssk, knit to 3 sts before marker, k2tog, k1, sm; k1, ssk, knit to last 3 sts, k2tog, k1—4 sts dec.

— Rep Dec Rnd every 3 rnds 4 more times—34 (42, 50, 58) sts.

— Knit 2 rnds.

— Graft heel sts.

— Turn sock RS out.

FINISHING

Weave in ends. Block as desired, being careful not to overstretch the sock.

CUFF-DOWN TWEED SOCKS

Design by
Fatimah Hinds

A PRIME EXAMPLE of Fatimah's inventive mind. What if a cable sock also has stripes? And contrasting toes? That's Cable C at left and Cable E on page 21 repeating all the way down through the toe, though of course you can choose any of the six cable options on pages 38–40.

The heel comes last here, a bit of grafting magic. We love the texture and color that comes from the tweed yarn, Serendipitous Wool's Agni T created by Shobha Nadarajah. Shobha is a wonderful hand dyer, and her palette is a lovely, subtle range of gently shifting color. Small batches mean that her yarn is a rare catch.

KNITTED MEASUREMENTS

Foot Circumference (measured at ball of foot): 7 (8.25, 9.25, 10.25)" [18 (21, 23.5, 26) cm]

Foot Length: 9 (10, 11, 11.5)" [23 (25.5, 28, 29) cm]

Leg Length: 6" (15 cm)

SIZES

1 (2, 3, 4)

MATERIALS

— Agni T by Serendipitous Wool [100 g skeins, each approx 231 yds (211 m), 85% superwash merino wool, 15% neps]: 1 (1, 2, 2) skein(s) (MC)

— Agni N by Serendipitous Wool [20 g skeins, each approx 49 yds (44 m), 75% superwash merino wool, 25% nylon]: 1 skein (CC)
    Colorway 1: Avenoir Teal Green (MC) and Funky Fuchsia (CC)
    Colorway 2: Meadowbrook (MC) and Winter's Heart (CC)

— Size US 5 (3.75 mm) double-point needles (set of 4 or 5), or size needed to achieve gauge

— Stitch markers

— Cable needle

— Waste yarn

GAUGE

23 sts and 32 rnds = 4" (10 cm) over rev st st

Note: Rev st st is not used for the entire sock. The cable pattern will draw the fabric in to the finished measurements.

STITCH PATTERN

2×2 Rib (multiple of 4 sts)

All Rnds: *K2, p2; rep from * to end.

NOTES

You may choose your cable pattern from among the six given on pages 38–40; they all have the same stitch multiple. The cable patterns may be worked from charts or written text.

The socks are worked from the cuff down. The sole and heel are worked in reverse stockinette so that the smooth side of the knitting is against the foot. The heel is worked inside out.

Traditional cable knitting calls for the use of a third needle, a short little cable needle. If you'd like to learn how to knit cables without a cable needle, which is faster and less fiddly, check out the videos from Emily and Alexa of Tin Can Knits.

LEG

- With MC, cast on 48 (56, 64, 70) sts. Join, being careful not to twist sts; pm for beg of rnd and work in the rnd as follows:
- Work in 2×2 Rib for 11 rnds. Purl 1 rnd.
- *Set-Up Rnd:* *K2 (4, 6, 4), pm, p2, [pm, k6, pm, p1] 2 (2, 2, 3) times, k2, p2, pm, k2 (4, 6, 4), pm for side; rep from * to end, omitting last pm.
- *Rnd 1:* *Knit to marker, sm, p2, [sm, work Cable Chart over 6 sts, sm, p1] 2 (2, 2, 3) times, k2, p2, sm, knit to marker, sm; rep from * to end.
- *Rnd 2:* *Knit to marker, sm, p2, [sm, work Cable Chart to marker, sm, p1] 2 (2, 2, 3) times, 1/1 LC, p2, sm, knit to marker, sm; rep from * to end.
- *Rnds 3–14:* Rep Rnds 1 and 2.
- *Rnd 15:* With CC, *knit to marker, sm, slip 2 wyib, [sm, work Cable Chart to marker, sm, slip 1 wyib] 2 (2, 2, 3) times, k2, slip 2 wyib, knit to marker, sm; rep from * to end.
- *Rnd 16:* *Knit to marker, sm, slip 2 wyib, [sm, work Cable Chart to marker, sm, slip 1 wyib] 2 (2, 2, 3) times, 1/1 LC, slip 2 wyib, knit to marker, sm; rep from * to end.
- Rep Rnds 1–16 once more.

HEEL OPENING

- *Next Rnd:* With MC, work in established pattern to side marker, sm, purl to end.
- *Next Rnd:* Work in established pattern to side marker, sm, drop working yarn and purl across sole sts with waste yarn, cut waste yarn; slide sole sts back to left needle and purl across sole sts with working yarn.

FOOT

- *Rnd 1:* *Knit to marker, sm, p2, [sm, work Cable Chart to marker, sm, p1] 2 (2, 2, 3) times, k2, p2, sm, knit to marker, sm, purl to end.
- *Rnd 2:* Knit to marker, sm, p2, [sm, work Cable Chart to marker, sm, p1] 2 (2, 2, 3) times, 1/1 LC, p2, sm, knit to marker, sm, purl to end.
- *Rnds 3–14:* Rep Rnds 1 and 2.
- *Rnd 15:* With CC, knit to marker, sm, slip 2 wyib, [sm, work Cable Chart to marker, sm, slip 1 wyib] 2 (2, 2, 3) times, k2, slip 2 wyib, knit to marker, sm, purl to end.
- *Rnd 16:* Knit to marker, sm, slip 2 wyib, [sm, work Cable Chart to marker, sm, slip 1 wyib] 2 (2, 2, 3) times, 1/1 LC, slip 2 wyib, knit to marker, sm], purl to end.

— Rep Rnds 1–16 until foot measures 5 (6, 7, 7.5)" [12.5 (15, 18, 19) cm], or to approx 4" (10 cm) less than desired length from waste yarn. Note: This allows for 2" (5 cm) each for toe and heel shaping.

TOE

— With CC, work in pattern to marker, sm, knit to end.

— *Rnd 1:* K1, ssk, work in pattern to 3 sts before side marker, k2tog, k1, sm, k1, ssk, knit to last 3 sts, k2tog, k1—4 sts dec.

— Continuing to work in pattern as established on instep sts and in st st on sole sts, rep Dec Rnd 1 every 3 rnds 3 more times—32 (40, 48, 54) sts.

— *Dec Rnd 2:* K1, ssk, knit to 3 sts before side marker, k2tog, k1, sm, k1, ssk, knit to last 3 sts, k2tog, k1—28 (36, 44, 50) sts.

— Knit 2 rnds.

— Graft toe sts (see page 41).

HEEL

— Turn the sock inside out. Carefully remove waste yarn and place 24 (28, 32, 35) top and bottom sts each onto 3 or 4 dpns. Rejoin MC to top sts; pm for beg of rnd and work in the rnd as follows:

— *Set-Up Rnd:* Knit to end of top sts, pick up and knit 1 st tbl from corner, pm, knit across bottom sts, pick up and knit 1 st tbl from corner—50 (58, 66, 72) sts.

— *Dec Rnd:* K1, ssk, knit to 3 sts before marker, k2tog, k1, sm; k1, ssk, knit to last 3 sts, k2tog, k1—4 sts dec.

— Rep Dec Rnd every 3 rnds 4 more times—30 (38, 46, 52) sts.

— Knit 2 rnds.

— Graft heel sts.

— Turn sock RS out.

FINISHING

Weave in ends. Block as desired, being careful not to overstretch the sock.

A small change makes an interesting variation. Eagle-eyed knitters will note that this sample is made without the slip stitches specified in the pattern—which means the maroon stripes are solid rather than broken up.

TOE-UP LACE SOCKS

Design by
Fatimah Hinds

WE BEGIN AT the toe, with a garter tab. A simple yarnover changes everything. All of a sudden, there's lace: modern and graphic, right there, worked along with cables. On page 22 is Cable F, where there are tiny cables inside a larger cable, and on page 25 is the simpler Cable D.

Either way, the cable pattern is offset, an asymmetry that makes for a pair of socks with a distinctive look. The pattern explains exactly how to place the cables for this unusual effect. The look of these could be pretty different if you go with another of the six cable options on pages 38–40.

The yarn is Pinto Bean from Lolabean Yarn Co. by Adella Colvin. Adella's vibrant colors and her famous speckles make these socks so much fun.

KNITTED MEASUREMENTS

Foot Circumference (measured at ball of foot): 7 (8.25, 9, 10)" [18 (21, 23, 25.5) cm]
Foot Length: 9 (10, 11, 11.5)" [23 (25.5, 28, 29) cm]
Leg Length: 5" (12.5 cm)

SIZES

1 (2, 3, 4)

MATERIALS

— Pinto Bean by Lolabean Yarn Co. [115 g skeins, each approx 250 yds (229 m), 100% merino wool]: 1 (2, 2, 2) skein(s) color Confetti or El Bosque
— Size US 5 (3.75 mm) double-point needles (set of 4 or 5), or size needed to achieve gauge
— Stitch markers
— Cable needle
— Waste yarn

GAUGE

23 sts and 32 rnds = 4" (10 cm) over rev st st
Note: Rev st st is not used for the entire sock. The cable pattern will draw the fabric in to the finished measurements.

NOTES

You may choose your cable pattern from among the six given on pages 38–40; they all have the same stitch multiple. The cable patterns may be worked from charts or written text.

The socks are worked from the toe up, beginning with a narrow panel at the tip of the toes, from which stitches are picked up to work in the round, with increases to shape the toe. The sole and heel are worked in reverse stockinette so that the smooth side of the knitting is against the foot. The heel is worked inside out.

Traditional cable knitting calls for the use of a third needle, a short little cable needle. If you'd like to learn how to knit cables without a cable needle, which is faster and less fiddly, check out the videos from Emily and Alexa of Tin Can Knits.

LEFT SOCK

TOE

— Cast on 9 (14, 16, 19) sts.

— Knit 8 rows.

— *Set-Up Row (RS):* K9 (14, 16, 19), pick up and knit 2 sts along left side edge (picking up in garter ridges), pm for side, pick up and knit another 2 sts along same side edge, 9 (14, 16, 19) sts across CO edge, then 2 sts along right side edge, pm for beg of rnd, pick up (but do not knit) 2 ridges along same side edge and place them on left needle—26 (36, 40, 46) sts.

Distribute sts among 3 or 4 dpns. Join and work in the rnd as follows:

— *Inc Rnd:* K2, M1R, knit to 2 sts before side marker, M1L, k2, sm, k2, M1R, knit to last 2 sts, M1L, k2—4 sts inc.

— Rep Inc Rnd 3 more times—42 (52, 56, 62) sts.

FOOT

— *Set-Up Rnd:* P1, k2, p2, pm, k2 (6, 6, 2), [kfb, k2] 1 (0, 0, 1) time(s), pm, p2, k2, pm, [p1, k1] 3 (5, 6, 8) times, p1, pm for side, purl to end—43 (52, 56, 63) sts.

- *Rnd 1:* P1, ssk, yo, p2, sm, work Cable Chart over 6 sts, sm, p2, yo, k2tog, sm, [p1, k1] 3 (5, 6, 8) times, p1, sm, purl to end.
- *Rnd 2:* P1, k2, p2, sm, work Cable Chart to marker, sm, p2, k2, sm, [p1, k1] 3 (5, 6, 8) times, p1, sm, purl to end.
- Rep Rnds 1 and 2 until foot measures 6.75 (7.75, 8.75, 8.75)" [17 (19.5, 22, 22) cm], or to approx 2.25" (5.5 cm) less than desired length, ending with Rnd 2.

HEEL OPENING

Next Rnd: Work in established pattern to side marker, sm, drop working yarn and purl across sole sts with waste yarn, cut waste yarn; slide sole sts back to left needle and purl across sole sts with working yarn.

LEG

- *Set-Up Rnd:* Work in pattern to side marker, remove marker, [k2tog] 1 (0, 0, 1) time(s), p1 (0, 0, 1), [k1, p1] 2 (6, 7, 7) times, pm, k2, p2, pm, work Cable Chart over 6 sts, pm, p2, k2—42 (52, 56, 62) sts.

Rnd 1: Work in pattern to third marker, sm, *p1, k1; rep from * to 1 st before marker, p1, sm, ssk, yo, p2, sm, work Cable Chart, sm, p2, yo, k2tog.

Rnd 2: Work in pattern to third marker, sm, *p1, k1; rep from * to 1 st before marker, p1, k2, p2, sm, work Cable Chart, sm, p2, k2.

Work even until leg measures 4" (10 cm) or to 1" (2.5 cm) less than desired length from waste yarn.

CUFF

Set-Up Rnd: P1, [k1, p1] twice, sm, work Cable Chart, sm, [p1, k1] twice, remove marker, *p1, k1; rep from * to 1 st before marker, p1, remove marker, [k1, p1] twice, sm, work Cable Chart, sm, [p1, k1] twice.

Next Rnd: Work Cable Chart between 2 sets of markers as established and work all sts outside of cable markers in rib pattern, as they appear.

Work even until cuff measures 1" (2.5 cm).

BO loosely in pattern.

HEEL

Turn the sock inside out. Carefully remove waste yarn and place 21 (26, 28, 31) top and bottom sts each onto 3 or 4 dpns. Rejoin yarn to top sts; pm for beg of rnd and work in the rnd as follows:

Set-Up Rnd: Knit to end of top sts, pick up and knit 1 st tbl from corner, knit across bottom sts, pick up and knit 1 st tbl from corner—44 (54, 58, 64) sts.

Dec Rnd: K1, ssk, knit to 3 sts before marker, k2tog, k1, sm; k1, ssk, knit to last 3 sts, k2tog, k1—4 sts dec.

Rep Dec Rnd every 3 rnds 4 more times—24 (34, 38, 44) sts.

Knit 2 rnds.

Graft heel sts (see page 41).

Turn sock RS out.

FINISHING

Weave in ends. Block as desired, being careful not to overstretch the sock.

RIGHT SOCK

Work as for left sock to end of toe—42 (52, 56, 62) sts.

FOOT

— *Set-Up Rnd:* P1, [k1, p1] 3 (5, 6, 8) times, k2, p2, pm, k2 (6, 6, 2), [kfb, k2] 1 (0, 0, 1) time(s), pm, p2, k2, p1, pm for side of foot, purl to end—43 (52, 56, 63) sts.

— *Rnd 1:* P1, [k1, p1] 3 (5, 6, 8) times, ssk, yo, p2, sm, work Cable Chart over 6 sts, sm, p2, yo, k2tog, p1, sm, purl to end.

— *Rnd 2:* P1, [k1, p1] 3 (5, 6, 8) times, k2, p2, sm, work Cable Chart to marker, sm, p2, k2, p1, sm, purl to end.

— Rep Rnds 1 and 2 until foot measures 6.75 (7.75, 8.75, 8.75)" [17 (19.5, 22, 22) cm], or to approx 2.25" (5.5 cm) less than desired length, ending with Rnd 2.

HEEL OPENING

Next Rnd: Work in established pattern to side marker, sm, drop working yarn and purl across sole sts with waste yarn, cut waste yarn; slide sole sts back to left needle and purl across sole sts with working yarn.

LEG

— *Set-Up Rnd:* Work in pattern to side marker, sm, k2, p2, pm, work Cable Chart over 6 sts, pm, p2, k2, pm, p1, [k2tog] 1 (0, 0, 1) time(s), *p1, k1; rep from * to end—42 (52, 56, 62) sts.

— *Rnd 1:* Work in pattern to side marker, sm, ssk, yo, p2, sm, work Cable Chart to marker, sm, p2, yo, k2tog, sm, *p1, k1; rep from * to end.

— *Rnd 2:* Work in pattern to side marker, sm, k2, p2, sm, work Cable Chart to markers, sm, p2, k2, *p1, k1; rep from * to end.

— Work even until leg measures 4 (4, 4.5, 4.5)" [10 (10, 11.5, 11.5) cm] or to 1" (2.5 cm) less than desired length from waste yarn.

CUFF

— *Set-Up Rnd:* P1, [k1, p1] 5 (7, 8, 10) times, sm, work Cable Chart to marker, sm, [p1, k1] twice, p1, remove marker, [k1, p1] twice, sm, work Cable Chart to marker, sm, *p1, k1; rep from * to end.

— *Next Rnd:* Work Cable Chart between 2 sets of markers as established and work all sts outside of cable markers in rib pattern, as they appear.

— Work even until cuff measures 1" (2.5 cm).

— BO loosely in pattern.

— Finish as for left sock.

TOE-UP KNEE SOCKS

Design by
Fatimah Hinds

TRULY SPECTACULAR. There's so much to love here. Fatimah starts us off at the toe, using her distinctive and very cool stockinette patch method. She then sets up the reverse stockinette sole.

The cables begin once the toe is complete, with Cables A and B shown here. Of course, you can choose your own cable from the six options on pages 38-40. From there it's a glorious ride to the top, where you can choose to shape the top of the calf or leave it simply ribbed.

The toe-up construction means you can try these on as you go, to get the perfect length and fit.

KNITTED MEASUREMENTS

Foot Circumference (measured at ball of foot): 6.75 (8, 9.25, 10.5)" [17 (20.5, 23.5, 26.5) cm]

Calf Circumference (measured at widest point): Calf Width 1: 11.75 (13, 14.25, 15.5)" [30 (33, 36, 39.5) cm]; Calf Width 2: 13 (14.25, 15.5, 16.5)" [33 (36, 39.5, 42) cm]

Foot Length: 9 (10, 11, 11.5)" [23 (25.5, 28, 29) cm]

Leg Length: 15 (15.5, 16, 16.5)" [38 (39.5, 40.5, 42) cm]

SIZES

1 (2, 3, 4)

MATERIALS

— Pinto Bean by Lolabean Yarn Co. [115 g skeins, each approx 250 yds (229 m), 100% merino wool]:
   2 (2, 3, 3) skeins color Strange Brew
   Note: This is enough yarn for either calf width and optional top-of-calf shaping.
— Size US 5 (3.75 mm) double-point needles (set of 4 or 5), or size needed to achieve gauge
— Stitch markers
— Waste yarn

GAUGE

23 sts and 32 rnds = 4" (10 cm) over rev st st

Note: Rev st st is not used for the entire sock. The cable pattern will draw the fabric in to the finished measurements.

NOTES

You may choose your cable pattern from among the six given on pages 38–40; they all have the same stitch multiple. The cable patterns may be worked from charts or written text.

The socks are worked from the toe up, beginning with a narrow panel at the tip of the toes, from which stitches are picked up to work in the round, with increases to shape the toe. The sole and heel are worked in reverse stockinette so that the smooth side of the knitting is against the foot. You have two options for calf width. The heel is worked inside out.

Traditional cable knitting calls for the use of a third needle, a short little cable needle. If you'd like to learn how to knit cables without a cable needle, which is faster and less fiddly, check out the videos of Emily and Alexa of Tin Can Knits.

TOE

— Cast on 8 (12, 16, 20) sts.

— Work 6 rows in st st, beg with a knit row.

— *Set-Up Row (RS):* K8 (12, 16, 20), pick up and knit 2 sts along left side edge, pm for side, pick up and knit another 2 sts along same side edge, 8 (12, 16, 20) sts across CO edge, then 2 sts along right side edge, pm for beg of rnd, pick up (but do not knit) 2 sts along same side edge and place them on left needle—24 (32, 40, 48) sts. Distribute sts among 3 or 4 dpns. Join and work in the rnd as follows:

— *Inc Rnd:* K2, M1R, knit to 2 sts before side marker, M1L, k2, sm, k2, M1R, knit to last 2 sts, M1L, k2—4 sts inc'd.

— Rep Inc Rnd every 3 rnds 4 more times—44 (52, 60, 68) sts.

FOOT

— *Set-Up Rnd:* P4 (6, 8, 10), pm, k6, pm, p2, pm, k6, pm, p4 (6, 8, 10), pm for side, purl to end.

— *Rnd 1:* Purl to marker, sm, work Cable Chart over 6 sts, sm, p2, sm, work Cable Chart over 6 sts, [sm, purl to marker] twice.

— Rep Rnd 1 until foot measures 6.75 (7.75, 8.75, 9.25)" [17 (19.5, 22, 23.5) cm], or to approx 2.25" (5.5 cm less than desired length.

HEEL OPENING

Next Rnd: Work in established pattern to side marker, sm, drop working yarn and purl across sole sts with waste yarn, cut waste yarn; slide sole sts back to left needle and purl across sole sts with working yarn.

LEG

— *Set-Up Rnd:* Work in pattern to side marker, sm, [k2, p2] 5 (6, 7, 8) times, k2.

— *Rnd 1:* Work to side marker, sm, *k2, p2; rep from * to last 2 sts, k2.

— Work even until leg measures 5.5 (6, 6.5, 7)" [14 (15, 16.5, 18) cm] from waste yarn.

SHAPE CALF

— *Rnd 1:* Work to side marker, sm, k1, pm, M1L, pm, k1, p2, *k2, p2; rep from * to last 2 sts, k1, pm, M1R, pm, k1—2 sts inc.

— *Rnds 2 and 3:* Work to side marker, [sm, k1] 3 times, work to 1 st before marker, [k1, sm] twice, k1.

— *Rnd 4:* Work to side marker, sm, k1, sm, knit to marker, M1L, sm, work to marker, sm, M1R, knit to marker, sm, k1—2 sts inc.

— *Rnds 5 and 6:* Work to side marker,

sm, k1, sm, knit to marker, sm, work to marker, sm, knit to marker, sm, k1.

— *Rnds 7–9:* Rep Rnds 4–6—2 sts inc.

— *Rnd 10:* Rep Rnd 4, removing markers between side marker and beg-of-rnd marker as you come to them—2 sts inc.

— Rep Rnds 1–10 three more times—76 (84, 92, 100) sts.

Calf Width 2 Only:

Rep Rnds 1–10 one more time—84 (92, 100, 108) sts.

Both Calf Widths:

Next Rnd: Work to side marker, sm, k2, *p2, k2; rep from * to end.

Note: After completing calf shaping, either shape top of calf to narrow width, or work to cuff without additional shaping.

If you want to omit additional top-of-calf shaping, rep last rnd until leg measures 14.25 (14.75, 15.25, 15.75)" [36 (37.5, 38.5, 40) cm], or approx .75" (2 cm) less than desired length from waste yarn, then proceed to Cuff.

If you want to work additional top-of-calf shaping, rep last rnd until leg measures 12.25 (12.75, 13.25, 13.75)" [31 (32.5, 33.5, 35) cm], or approx 2.75" (7 cm) less than desired length from waste yarn.

Shape Top of Calf (optional)

— *Rnd 1:* Work to side marker, sm, work 15 sts, k2tog, k1, pm, work to last 18 sts, pm, k1, ssk, work to end—2 sts dec.
— *Rnd 2:* Work to end.
— *Rnd 3:* Work to 3 sts before 2nd marker, k2tog, k1, sm, work to marker, sm, k1, ssk, work to end—2 sts dec.
— *Rnd 4:* Work to end.
— Rep Rnds 3 and 4 six more times—60 (68, 76, 84) sts for calf width 1 or 68 (76, 84, 92) sts for calf width 2.

CUFF

— *Rnds 1–4:* Work to end.
— *Rnds 5 and 6:* *P1, k1-tbl; rep from * to end.
— BO loosely in pattern.

HEEL

— Turn the sock inside out. Carefully remove waste yarn and place 22 (26, 30, 34) top and bottom sts each onto 3 or 4 dpns. Rejoin yarn to top sts; pm for beg of rnd and work in the rnd as follows:
— *Set-Up Rnd:* Knit to end of top sts, pick up and knit 1 st tbl from corner, knit across bottom sts, pick up and

knit 1 st tbl from corner—46 (54, 62, 70) sts.
— *Dec Rnd:* K1, ssk, knit to 3 sts before marker, k2tog, k1, sm; k1, ssk, knit to last 3 sts, k2tog, k1—4 sts dec.
— Rep Dec Rnd every 3 rnds 4 more times—26 (34, 42, 50) sts.
— Knit 2 rnds.
— Graft heel sts (see page 41).
— Turn sock RS out.

FINISHING

Weave in ends. Block as desired, being careful not to overstretch the sock.

Cable C

CABLE GUIDE

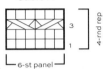

Cable A

Cable C (panel of 6 sts)

— *Rnd 1:* K2, 2/2 RC.
— *Rnd 2:* K6.
— *Rnd 3:* 2/2 RC, k2.
— *Rnds 4–6:* K6.
— Rep Rnds 1–6 for pattern.

Cable A (panel of 6 sts)

— *Rnds 1 and 2:* K6.
— *Rnd 3:* 1/2 RC, 1/2 LC.
— *Rnd 4:* K6.
— Rep Rnds 1–4 for pattern.

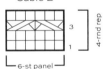

Cable B

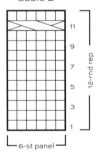

Cable D

Cable B (panel of 6 sts)

— *Rnds 1 and 2:* K6.
— *Rnd 3:* 1/2 LC, 1/2 RC.
— *Rnd 4:* K6.
— Rep Rnds 1–4 for pattern.

Cable D (panel of 6 sts)

— *Rnds 1–10:* K6.
— *Rnd 11:* 3/3 LC.
— *Rnd 12:* K6.
— Rep Rnds 1–12 for pattern.

Cable E

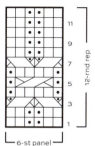

12-rnd rep

6-st panel

Cable F

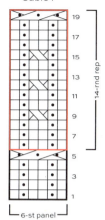

14-rnd rep

6-st panel

Cable E (panel of 6 sts)

— *Rnds 1 and 2:* K2, p2, k2.
— *Rnd 3:* 2/1 LPC, 2/1 RPC.
— *Rnd 4:* P1, k4, p1.
— *Rnd 5:* P1, 2/2 RC, p1.
— *Rnd 6:* P1, k4, p1.
— *Rnd 7:* 2/1 RPC, 2/1 LPC.
— *Rnds 8–12:* K2, p2, k2.
— Rep Rnds 1–12 for pattern.

	Knit
•	Purl
⟩⟨	1/1 LC
	1/2 LC
	1/2 RC
	2/1 LPC
	2/1 RPC
	2/2 RC
	3/3 LC
	3/3 RRC

Cable F (panel of 6 sts)

— *Rnds 1–4:* K1, p1, k2, p1, k1.
— *Rnd 5:* 3/3 RRC.
— *Rnds 6–8:* K1, p1, k2, p1, k1.
— *Rnd 9:* K1, p1, 1/1 LC, p1, k1.
— *Rnds 10–11:* K1, p1, k2, p1, k1.
— *Rnds 12–17:* Rep Rnds 9–11 twice.
— *Rnd 18:* K1, p1, k2, p1, k1.
— *Rnd 19:* 3/3 RRC.
— Rep Rnds 6–19 for pattern.

See explanations of cable abbreviations on page 40.

CABLE ABBREVIATIONS

1/1 LC (1 over 1 Left Cross): Slip the next stitch to cable needle and hold at front of work, k1, k1 from cable needle.

1/2 LC (1 over 2 Left Cross): Slip the next stitch to cable needle and hold at front of work, k2, k1 from cable needle.

1/2 RC (1 over 2 Right Cross): Slip the next 2 stitches to cable needle and hold at back of work, k1, k2 from cable needle.

2/1 LPC (2 over 1 Left Purl Cross): Slip the next 2 stitches to cable needle and hold at front of work, p1, k2 from cable needle.

2/1 RPC (2 over 1 Right Purl Cross): Slip the next stitch to cable needle and hold at back of work, k2, p1 from cable needle.

2/2 RC (2 over 2 Right Cross): Slip the next 2 stitches to cable needle and hold at back of work, k2, k2 from cable needle.

3/3 LC (3 over 3 Left Cross): Slip the next 3 stitches to cable needle and hold at front of work, k3, k3 from cable needle.

3/3 RRC (3 over 3 Right Ribbed Cross): Slip the next 3 stitches to cable needle and hold at back of work, k1, p1, k1, (k1, p1, k1) from cable needle.

GRAFTING

Using a blunt tapestry needle, thread a length of yarn
approximately 4 times the length of the section to be joined.
With stitches still on the needles, hold the pieces to be joined
parallel, with WSs together, both needle tips pointing to the right.
Working from right to left:

Setup
—   Insert tapestry needle into first stitch on front needle
     purlwise, pull yarn through, leaving stitch on needle.
—   Insert tapestry needle into first stitch on back needle
     knitwise, pull yarn through, leaving stitch on needle.

Repeat for all stitches
—   *Insert tapestry needle into first stitch on front needle
     knitwise, pull yarn through, remove stitch from needle.
—   Insert tapestry needle into next stitch on front needle
     purlwise, pull yarn through, leave stitch on needle.
—   Insert tapestry needle into first stitch on back needle
     purlwise, pull yarn through, remove stitch from needle.
—   Insert tapestry needle into next stitch on back needle
     knitwise, pull yarn through, leave stitch on needle.
—   Repeat from *, adjusting stitch tension every 3 or 4 stitches
     to match the pieces being joined.
—   When 1 stitch remains on each needle, cut yarn and pass
     through last 2 stitches to fasten off.

MEET FATIMAH HINDS

A prolific knitwear designer, Fatimah Hinds loves to teach. For years, she was in the classroom with middle school math students. Now, she devotes her teaching skills to knitting and also to justice, equity, and anti-racism in the knitting world.

Fatimah explains her mission on her website, DisturbingTheFleece.com: "I noticed that there weren't too many members of the fiber community that looked like me. I knew there were makers of all races and identities but we were hard to find. I was inspired to take up more space on purpose. It is important to me to bring my full self

to the table. My goal: to inspire others to be their true selves and to build a community of lifelong learners that is welcoming and inclusive of all identities but particularly marginalized ones." We all need to listen to her message, and to heed Maya Angelou's famous imperative to know better, and do better.

You'll find Fatimah on Instagram @disturbingthefleece. She is a teacher in Season 7 of Knit Stars. And her designs—sweaters, accessories, and even more socks!—are available on Disturbingthefleece.com.

You've made your way from middle school teacher to knitwear designer, with over 100 designs to your credit. Do you still draw on your background in math and earth sciences?
I don't think that teaching knitting and designing knitwear are different than what I did before, as much as they may seem like it on paper. I'm still teaching people something they didn't know. I'm still inviting them to be a little uncomfortable. I'm still trying to give them all the tools they need to be successful. So there's actually a decent amount of overlap. To be an effective teacher, you have

to be creative in how you present the material, and you have to be open to new ideas. That's important to me with my knitting community and my social media community, to be a learner, too.

I really miss teaching middle schoolers. They're delightful.

Cables are clearly one of your passions. How do you design them?

It's trial and error, it's mental gymnastics, it's reverse engineering. I create cables in my mind, and then I try them out with yarn and needles. I really love looking at commercial sweaters and reverse engineering cables.

How did you arrive at the six cables in this Field Guide?

It was important that they were visually different. And important that the cables did not get obscured by the yarn—I was working with hand-dyed yarn and tweed yarn with neps, those fluffy bits. They had to play nice together.

What's your advice to someone who has never tried cables?

A cable is just stitches knit in a different order. That's all. There's nothing scary.

What are your top tips for a knitter who's getting started knitting socks?

Yarn and gauge. For the best chance at durability, choose yarn with lots of plies and knit the socks on a tighter gauge. Resist the urge to use the largest suggested needle size.

Start toe up. If you're new to your sock journey, I would start toe up. When you knit toe up, you can try it on your foot and check the fit the whole time. If you're going top down, you can't do that.

Negative ease. It's part of how you make a sock feel good inside your shoes—make it maybe a quarter of an inch shorter than the length of your foot and narrower than your actual foot circumference. A sock with positive ease can cause bunching under the foot. Some people don't have the mobility to put on a sock with negative ease, so for them, that's not feasible.

Fit. With the afterthought heel, you can try on your whole sock. After taking out the waste yarn, you put those stitches on needles to knit the heel, and you can actually put that sock on and see what needs to happen with the fit. Do I need extra rounds? Or less?

ABBREVIATIONS

Approx: Approximately

Beg: Begin(ning)(s)

BO: Bind off

Cn: Cable needle

CO: Cast on

Dec: Decreas(ed)(es)(ing)

Dpn: Double-pointed needle(s)

Inc: Increas(ed)(es)(ing)

K: Knit

K2tog: Knit 2 stitches together. One stitch has been decreased.

Kfb: Knit into the front and back of next stitch. One stitch has been increased.

M1L: (Make 1 left) Insert left needle from front to back under horizontal strand between stitch just worked and the next stitch on the left needle. Knit this strand through the back loop. One stitch has been increased.

M1R: (Make 1 right) Insert left needle from back to front under horizontal strand between stitch just worked and the next stitch on the left needle. Knit this strand through the front loop. One stitch has been increased.

P: Purl

Pm: Place marker

Rep: Repeat(ed)(ing)(s)

Rev st st: Reverse stockinette stitch

Rnd(s): Round(s)

RS: Right side

Sl: Slip

Sm: Slip marker

Ssk: Slip 1 stitch knitwise, slip 1 stitch purlwise, insert left needle into the front of these 2 stitches and knit them together from this position. One stitch has been decreased.

St st: Stockinette stitch

St(s): Stitch(es)

Tbl: Through the back loop(s)

Tog: Together

WS: Wrong side

Wyib: With yarn in back

Yo: Yarnover